Living the Elijah Project

By: Andrea M. Polnaszek, LCSW

Living the Elijah Project

© 2018 by Andrea M. Polnaszek

Artwork created by Matthew Reddy

Assistant to the author: Renee Wurzer

Unless otherwise indicated, all Scripture taken from the Holy Bible, NEW INTERNATIONAL VERSION ®. Copyright © 1973, 1978, 1984, 2011 by Biblica, Inc. All rights reserved worldwide. Used by permission.

Printed in the United States of America

ISBN: 978-1-7329-8241-3

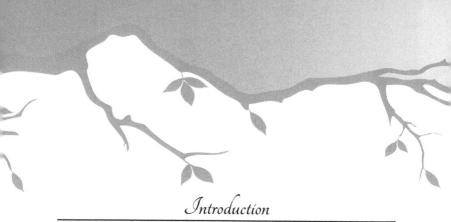

Introduction

It's been years since I began my journey with Elijah. I often tell people that I didn't find Elijah – his story found me. I find great solace in the fact that a legendary prophet like Elijah became overwhelmed, tapped out, and exhausted. When I began this journey I was at a personal low in my life. I was a resentful servant who didn't like her reflection in the mirror. Since that time, I have been blessed in sharing my reflections on Elijah's journey with hundreds of people. I believe in the principles of God's protection and provision, while realizing that real life circumstances make it hard to believe sometimes. I often find myself standing in the middle of my kitchen, stomping my feet, trying to find my breath – and I wonder, where is all that great "elijah project" stuff in me?

The Elijah Project book and workbook give us a starting point, a common language for the journey, and an understanding of how to find out what is going on inside.

Living the Elijah Project is the next step – it uses our common understanding to help us apply the protection and provision principals in everyday life. I chose to write this in 40 bite-sized pieces because Elijah's story is full of 40 day mini-adventures. God uses 40 days, weeks, months, and years throughout His story with His people. Today, the current philosophy on good habit forming says it takes 30 days to form a new habit. I believe 40 days just gives us the extra *Umff* to own the habit or pattern of *Living the Elijah Project*.

I trust you will find hope and peace and God's protection and provision.

Begin with the End in Mind

The LORD said, "Go out and stand on the mountain in the presence of the LORD, for the LORD is about to pass by."
– *1 Kings 19:11*

The late Dr. Stephen Covey's *2nd Habit* says: "Begin with the end in mind." His philosophy: "to begin with the end in mind is to begin with the image of the end of your life as a frame of reference by which everything else is measured." If you don't have a clear vision for where you are going, you will never get there. Elijah's story spans four chapters of Scripture in *1 Kings*. There are many mini-adventures within his BIG story. It seems appropriate for us to know where we are going with Elijah.

The Lord invites Elijah to stand on the mountain in His presence. This is an incredible invitation – a request that even a non-believer might want to take part in. As we embark on Elijah's journey with him, we will quickly recognize that each stop along the way prepared a pathway for him to see God!

We hope for the same thing. When we begin to record the stops on our personal journey we believe God will reveal a bigger picture of Himself *in* us.

When you get to the end, how do you want your story to read?

Dear God,

I get so caught up in the little steps I take each day. I rarely step back to see how you are weaving my foot prints together to make a path. Lord, help me to see my journey as part of a bigger cosmic journey that connects you with your people for eternity. Amen

Day 2

Who is Elijah?

Now Elijah the Tishbite, from Tishbe in Gilead, said to Ahab, "As the LORD, the God of Israel, lives, whom I serve, there will be neither dew nor rain in the next few years except at my word."
– 1 Kings 17:1

Elijah was a prophet whose name meant: *Yahweh is God.* He was a Tishbite living in Gilead, a rough man who probably worked the land. Elijah's very name signaled to those around him that he honored the one true God. His name means God. We all have a name, a story, a personality, and an origin. Elijah was a man called by God to be part of many miraculous and incredible things. He was called to *stand in the gap* between God and His people during a time when Israel had wandered far from God.

As Christ followers we are called to *stand in the gap* between Christ and His people – sharing the good news of Jesus with others.

Who are you called to stand in the gap for: your husband, your daughter, a friend, or a co-worker?

Dear God,

Your prophet Elijah is an inspiration. He reminds me that I have a responsibility to *stand in the gap* for those who need you! Lord, lead me to someone who needs you today. Open my eyes to see and hear their need. Open my heart to share your love with them. Amen

Day 3

Who am I?

You have searched me, LORD,
  and you know me.
You know when I sit and when I rise;
  you perceive my thoughts from afar.
You discern my going out and my lying down;
  you are familiar with all my ways.
Before a word is on my tongue you,
  LORD, know it completely.
– Psalm 139:1-4

Do you know what your name means? In ancient times a name conveyed personal characteristics about its holder. It indicated your family heritage and even whom you worshiped. This is still true today. I married a man from Polish descent. Our last name lets everyone know where his family hails from.

Take a moment to think about how you are doing today. What are you excited about and what are you afraid of? Close your eyes and scan your body from head to toe, where are you holding tension or elation? Release your shoulders and let your arms fall by your sides. Count to 40 slowly. Reflect on how you feel after giving yourself a momentary break!

Elijah's name means *Yahweh is God*. Think of all the hats you wear: mother, father, sister, brother, son, daughter, co-worker, neighbor, and friend. When you think about yourself – what message does your life convey?

Dear God,

You can see all of me, both inside and out. Your word says that I am fearfully and wonderfully made. Lord, I pray that you would remind me of who I am in your eyes and give me the courage to share that with others. Amen

What's Elijah's Story?

Then the word of the LORD came to Elijah: "Leave here, turn eastward and hide in the Kerith Ravine, east of the Jordan." – *1 Kings 17:2-3*

Elijah was a Tishbite from the land of Gilead. Tishbites were hardworking people who herded flocks and worked the land. The land of Gilead can't even be traced on a map today. Elijah was from an insignificant place. He didn't have name, or title, or education. And the God of Abraham, Isaac, and Jacob called him to leave his homeland and bring a message to the king of Samaria.

Elijah boldly told King Ahab there was going to be a drought and God directed Elijah to live in the Kerith Valley. It is hard to comprehend from our Western perspective the Sovereignty of a King. King Ahab had "off with his head" kind of power. Elijah's story had pressed him to courageously follow God and boldly journey to a new, remote land.

Elijah didn't question God when He told him to move to the Kerith Valley. He went and that very obedience saved his life. The remote land was kept hidden from the king's army and in this way God protected Elijah from certain death.

Dear God,

Open my ears to hear the message of God like Elijah did. Give me the courage to stand up to my enemy and share the truth of God with those you ask me to. May you be the conductor of my life story. Amen

What's Your Story?

> I praise you because *I am fearfully and wonderfully made*; your works are wonderful, I know that full well
> – *Psalm 139:14 emphasis added*

Elijah was a prophet of God from the land of Gilead. God uniquely equipped him with a tough skin to do a tough job. God creates and calls His people to do wonderful works. This is how God gets things done.

God speaks in a still small voice and gives you little directions that grow into bigger directives. Recently I had someone come to my mind. I simply texted my friend and found out that in the moment I was writing my message something really terrible had happened in her life. We all have choices. We can listen to the promptings and act on them, even if they seem weird, or inconvenient, or we can let them go. I believe God works whether we act or not. The cool thing is that He gives us an opportunity to be part of amazing adventures when we stop to listen and obey.

Have you ever felt prompted to do something, to call someone, to ask someone out for coffee, or to give someone a gift? What was it and when was the last time you did it?

Dear God,

It is so hard to see how you can take all things and work them out for my good and your glory, but I know you promise that. Please help me see your hand even in the most difficult points of my journey. Amen

The Brook

"Leave here, turn eastward and hide in the Kerith Ravine, east of the Jordan. You will drink from the brook, and I have ordered the ravens to feed you there."
– 1 Kings 17:3-4

After Elijah delivered the message to King Ahab: *Surely for three years no dew will hit the ground,* God immediately directs him to the Kerith Valley where ravens are commanded to bring him bread and meat in the morning and evening and he has access to a bubbling brook.

Did you ever stop to think about what kind of meat the ravens brought Elijah? I guess I always thought they were finger sandwiches: roast beef, ham, or maybe tuna. Well, they weren't delectable little morsels. Ravens are scavengers and probably brought him road kill. Elijah was out in the wilderness fed by scavengers for some time. I imagine he and God became pretty tight.

God's provisions don't always look the way we expect. When Elijah stepped out in faith and obedience, I bet he didn't expect God's provision to be a desolate spot by a brook, where he was alone with ravens delivering him sun dried meat. And yet, it is unmistakable that God protected and provided for Elijah. He kept him safe from King Ahab's armies and provided him food and water in the time of a drought.

Dear God,

It's hard for me to see your provision sometimes. You don't always give me what I want or even what I think I need. Lord, please open my eyes to see how you are taking care of me today. Amen

Day 7

The Brook Dried Up

Some time later the brook dried up because there had been no rain in the land. – 1 Kings 17:7

Elijah moved in the Kerith Valley. He set himself up to live there, literally living on the land and waiting for his needs to be met by God through birds. The Bible says: *Some time later the brook dried up*. Elijah couldn't live without water. When the brook dried up and God delivered His next direction, Elijah followed God's word. It sounds so simple for Elijah. He had no more water, so he got up and moved to a new place where he believed God would protect and provide for him.

I don't think it was any easier for Elijah to move from his familiar surroundings in the valley, than it is for us to follow the *still small voice* that prompts us to obey God today.

Where is the brook dried up in your life? Have you moved, or are you waiting for the water to come back?

18

Dear God,

Move in the depths of my being. Change my heart to truly trust that your provision and protection are what I need, even when it is not what I want. May I see your hand work in my life and may I follow your directions. Amen

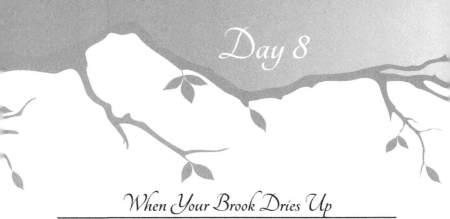

Day 8

When Your Brook Dries Up

"Whoever believes in me, as Scripture has said, rivers of
living water will flow from within them."
– *John 7:38 emphasis added*

Just like Elijah, there are things in your life that have dried
up. The circumstances of life often leave you wanting more,
or not ready to say goodbye. In Elijah's story moving on and
following God's direction was necessary for survival. He
was living through a drought, without water he would die.
Sometimes the things that dry up in our lives are not life or
death, so it is easy to hang on and not release them to God.

I think if I were Elijah I may have waited for another drop of
water in the brook, or dug deeper into the creek bed looking
for a hidden spring. I really don't like change and many times I
allow things to linger longer than they should.

Grief is a difficult process. The American tradition of grief is
short and succinct. We pay our respects, bury the dead, and
share a meal. Within three days of the loss we are expected
to go back to work and resume regular life. If that is how we
handle the death of a person, it is no wonder that we don't
grieve the everyday losses like: job layoff, kids graduating, and
the empty nest.

Closing Activity

December

Friends from the church - Helen, Don + Diane
Rhondi, Sheila, Susan + Roland,
Rich + Ashley, Jim + Dee Dee,
Vicki + Blan, George + Diana,
Stan - Juanita

Close your eyes and imagine three things you have lost in the past six months. Now with your eyes closed count to 40.

Open your eyes and reimagine those losses.

Has your perspective changed?

Georgie ☺
Food obsession
Addiction

Dear God,

It is so hard to let go. Please help me to open my hands and release what I am trying to control. And then Lord, allow me to see what you have filled my hands with in return! Fill me up so I can pour out your love on others. Amen

Satan be silent - Lord be Loud!

Day 9

Gathering Sticks

"Go at once to Zarephath in the region of Sidon and stay there. I have directed a widow there to supply you with food." So he went to Zarephath. When he came to the town gate, a widow was there gathering sticks. He called to her and asked, "Would you bring me a little water in a jar so I may have a drink?" – *1 Kings 17:9-10*

When we meet the widow, she is inside the city gate gathering sticks. Elijah asks her to bring him some water and a cake of bread. She responds to him with genuine concern and the reality of her limits.

"I don't have any bread—only a handful of flour in a jar and a little olive oil in a jug." – *1 Kings 17:12*

Have you ever been asked to give something that you didn't have to give? It might have been money, or time that someone desperately needed. You were tapped out and you didn't have anything left to give. This is where the widow found herself. Elijah's need revealed her want.

Our human tendency is to try to give even when it is not ours to give. The most priceless lesson is to trust God as the Giver and send the requests of others back to Him. It is amazing how completely God provides when we trust Him.

Where are you trying to provide for yourself? How can you release that need for control to God today?

Dear God,

I feel worn out from giving. Please help me rely on you and not myself to care for the needs of others. Today remind me to stop and ask for your help instead of *taking care of business* in my own strength. And when you provide may I acknowledge you as the Giver. Amen

Don't Be Afraid

> Elijah said to her, "Don't be afraid. Go home and do as you have said. But first make a small loaf of bread for me from what you have and bring it to me, and then make something for yourself and your son. For this is what the LORD, the God of Israel, says: 'The jar of flour will not be used up and the jug of oil will not run dry until the day the LORD sends rain on the land.'" – *1 Kings 17:13-14*

Elijah asked the widow for more. After he asked her for water and a cake of bread, she said: "I don't have it to give." And with audacious faith Elijah asked her for water and bread again. I can't imagine how afraid the widow must have been to share her last resources with a stranger, but she did it. The widow obeyed God.

Scarcity is a mindset. When we live in the light of comparison, there will always be someone with more. The equal and opposite is true as well, when we live in the light of comparison, there will always be someone with less. We often notice the one with more, rather than then the one with less. The widow is a shining example of childlike faith. She obeyed God and believed that He would take care of her if she did as He asked. And He did!

Wherever you are sitting or standing to read this page, quietly look to your left and then to your right. Who do you see? Imagine the pain or want within the person sitting next to you. Imagine your greatest loss and most significant pain and realize that your closest neighbor has felt his/her own pain to that level.

Dear God,

I ask you to bind up the wounds of the broken hearted. As the writer of *Isaiah* put it *may my healing come* as I lift up the pain of my neighbor. Amen

Enough

For the jar of flour was not used up and the jug of oil did
not run dry, in keeping with the word of the LORD spoken
by Elijah. – *1 Kings 17:16*

Not only did the widow give Elijah water and bread, she
brought him home and he lived with her for some time.
The story chronicles God's daily provision. We often recall the
BIG miracles in our lives: the check which came in the mail to
cover our extraordinary heat bill, the just-in-the-nick-of-time
job offer, or the mechanic who absorbed the cost of fixing our
car. But, do we ever account for all the little miracles, like food,
water, and a roof over our heads? We take for granted those
provisions every day.

Every day when the widow went back to her pantry, there was
just enough oil and just enough flour to make another loaf of
bread. Her jars never overflowed, the provision came up from
the bottom, never running dry. God's provisions are often like
this and His people often overlook those gifts. May we be an
up from the bottom people.

How has God provided just enough for you today?

Dear God,

Thank you for providing for me. Thank you for giving me just
enough food to feed my family, just enough gas for my car,
and most of all just enough energy for another day. Lord, help
me recognize your protection and provision in my life today!
Amen

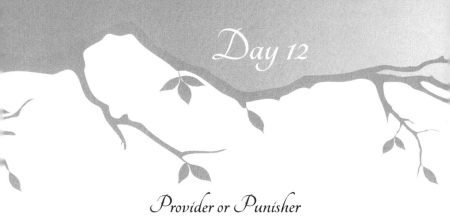

Day 12

Provider or Punisher

Some time later the son of the woman who owned the house became ill. He grew worse and worse, and finally stopped breathing. She said to Elijah, "What do you have against me, man of God? Did you come to remind me of my sin and kill my son?" – *1 Kings 17:17-18*

Elijah, the widow, and her son all enjoyed God's provision of hot bread every day for some time; until one day when the widow's son became so ill *his breath left him*. He died. Every day, the widow had watched God provide flour and oil. But on this day, it wasn't provision she watched, it was deep withdrawal, the death of her only son. The widow did not mask her grief, she lashed out at Elijah. She accused God of punishing her for her past sins.

Elijah doesn't say a word. He gathers up the boy and carries him upstairs. Some Biblical narratives say Elijah took him to the roof, others record he took him to an upstairs bedroom. But they all agree that Elijah prayed. He lay on top of the boy three times and prayed that God would bring his life back.

And then, in the stillness of an upper room, *the boy's breath came back*. The widow's response was to declare: "God you are the God." It was a miracle, no other explanation. Her son was dead and now he was alive.

Is there anything in your life that feels dead? Do you wish it were alive? Any place where you question if God is punishing you for your past mistakes, missteps, or sins?

Dear God,

I often wonder if you look down on me and see only my failings. I wonder if you are waiting to pounce on my mistakes. Please help me to see you as my heavenly Father, who longs to pick me up, cover me up, and bring *my breath back to me*. Amen

Day 13

Widows

Adam and his wife were both naked, and they felt no shame. – Genesis 2:25

In ancient times a woman's only connection with community was through a man. First a father and then she was given to a husband. If her husband died, her next connection was a son or maybe a brother. Elijah's widow had no husband, but her son kept her drawn into community.

I wonder if the widow's breath left her too, when her boy died. Did she gasp for air as she watched her son take his last sip? And then when she choked her breath back up ... the only words she found were bitter. She was instantly in a wash of shame and internally isolated from her Provider.

I love that Elijah didn't say a word. I love that he gathered her precious connector in his arms and ran up the stairs to lay him before God. And I love that the widow followed him. After her shaming outburst, she flew into action waiting expectantly to see what this Man of God would do.

God is not the author of shame, Satan is. Adam and Eve walked the Garden of Eden naked and unashamed. Their desire for God-like status caused sin and shame to enter the world.

What do you feel like when that wash of shame comes?

When you question how your past is influencing your future, remember that God is your Protector and Provider. He is working all things together for good for those called according to His purpose.

Dear God,

Today I pray that you would replace my regret with relief. I pray that you would help me open my hands so you can fill them. I pray that you might connect me to your Holy Spirit so my very breath is in step with yours. Amen

Day 14

Drought

After a long time, in the third year, the word of the LORD
came to Elijah: "Go and present yourself to Ahab, and
I will send rain on the land." So Elijah went to present
himself to Ahab.
– 1 Kings 18:1-2

Take delight in the Lord,
  and he will give you the desires of your heart.
Commit your way to the Lord;
  trust in him and he will do this:
– Psalm 37:4-5

There was absolutely no rain in Samaria for three
years. It is hard to imagine a drought. Most towns and
communities have water tower store houses. Even when the
authorities recommend a water ban, most of us can still use
water to drink, bath, and keep the household going. The land
of Samaria did not see rain or dew for three whole years. This
is a significant experience.

While I may not be able to imagine a drought from water ...
I can imagine a drought with God. I've lived through prayer
life droughts, times when I prayed and prayed and prayed for
God to do something in my life and He didn't seem to answer.
When I was in college I prayed and prayed and prayed for
someone to fall in love with me. I earnestly prayed year after
year, and my prayer was not answered.

Then one night while driving through a rainstorm, God said:
"Why don't you pray for what I want, instead of what you want?"
He told me that *Psalm 37:4* wasn't about my desires but His

desires for me! God used a rainstorm to end my prayer drought. He asks us to follow His ways, then He promises us the desires of our hearts.

What are the desires of your heart?

Dear God,

I want to delight in you and trust that you will give me the desires of my heart. Help me to commit my way to you. Amen

Day 15

What Are You Famous For?

As Obadiah was walking along, Elijah met him. Obadiah recognized him, bowed down to the ground, and said, "Is it really you, my lord Elijah?" "Yes," he replied. "Go tell your master, 'Elijah is here.'" – *1 Kings 18:7-8*

Elijah set out on his journey to tell the king the drought was going to end. On his way he runs into the king's *right hand man*, Obadiah. Obadiah knows who Elijah is and bows down in honor of this Man of God. Imagine being famous for your faith. Imagine people knowing you because of the BIG things you had done for God. Elijah is that man. He is known for his bold march to tell King Ahab that a drought was coming.

When we are marked by the blood of Jesus, we are set apart from the world. The people of God look different from the people of the world. Our life goals, our way of being, our actions should lead to a life of integrity. Our spirit is to be of LOVE. Does your family know you are a Christian because your actions are different? Do your co-workers or your boss know that your work actions are different, even risky because you seek to honor God first and your boss second? If not, now is the time to bow down and ask God to make your life look different.

Do people know you are a Christian because your actions are different even risky because you seek to honor God first?

34

Dear God, We ask you to make our lives look different

May the fragrance of my being smell of You not of me. May
people see me coming and know that I am your child. Lord,
come and live in me and change who I am and how I look to
the world. Amen

Shame

"Oh, sir," Obadiah protested, "what harm have I done to you that you are sending me to my death? For I swear by God that the king has searched every nation and kingdom on earth from end to end to find you. And each time when he was told 'Elijah isn't here,' King Ahab forced the king of that nation to swear to the truth of his claim. And now you say, 'Go and tell him Elijah is here'! But as soon as I leave you, the Spirit of the LORD will carry you away, who knows where, and when Ahab comes and can't find you, he will kill me; yet I have been a true servant of the LORD all my life. Has no one told you about the time when Queen Jezebel was trying to kill the LORD's prophets, and I hid a hundred of them in two caves and fed them with bread and water? And now you say, 'Go tell the king that Elijah is here'! Sir, if I do that, I'm dead!"
– 1 Kings 18:9-1 TLB

Obadiah bowed low to the ground in honor of Elijah. And in the next breath he questioned what he had done wrong and feared for his life. When we truly take up our cross and follow what Jesus asks of us, it often leads to tricky and challenging circumstances – tight spaces that God can only get us out of.

Elijah asked Obadiah to tell King Ahab that the drought was coming to an end. Obadiah responded with an echo of the widow: *Oh, what have I done wrong?* God's big plans left both Obadiah and the widow doubting God's provision and protection. Obadiah rehearsed all the good he had done for God. He desperately tried to remind God through Elijah of his obedience. There is no doubt that Obadiah questioned whether God could see him in that scary moment. And then, with all his racing thoughts and questions, Obadiah obeyed. Just like the widow, Obadiah first questioned and then recanted, obeying God's command.

How has God asked you to obey him today?

Dear God,

I can't see how you will work my present circumstances out for my good. In fact, I know what you have asked me to do and I am resisting because I doubt your provision and protection. Lord, renew my strength and reignite my vision for you. Give me the courage to take one step in your direction. Amen

The Blame Game

> But Elijah said, "I swear by the Lord God of the armies
> of heaven, in whose presence I stand, that I will present
> myself to Ahab today." So Obadiah went to tell Ahab
> that Elijah had come; and Ahab went out to meet him.
> "So it's you, is it?—the man who brought this disaster
> upon Israel!" Ahab exclaimed when he saw him. "You're
> talking about yourself," Elijah answered. "For you and
> your family have refused to obey the LORD and have
> worshiped Baal instead." – *1 Kings 18:15-18 TLB*

Elijah reassured Obadiah of God's protection. He swore the
protection of God's angels on him. And Obadiah obeyed.
Obadiah told King Ahab that the drought was going to end,
and Obadiah lived.

What a greeting Elijah receives! King Ahab says, *so here is the
guy that has brought ruin (famine) to my kingdom.* When King
Ahab accuses Elijah of ruining his kingdom, Elijah doesn't own
any of the statements. He retorts with truth. Elijah reminds
Ahab that it is his own disobedience to God that caused the
problems for Israel. He stands firmly in the truth that his *God
is the* God and does not waver.

The normal human posture in response to an unfair or
unwanted accusation is to defend. Blaming words instigate
a defensive answer. Have you ever had someone approach
you with blame? The first thing out of their mouth is an
accusation. Think for a moment ... what happens inside you?
Does your stomach feel sick? What races through your mind?

Dear God,

I so often defend my behavior. Help me to hide your Word in my heart ... so that your words flow from me and not my own. Lord, help me to hide in the shadow of your wings and not respond defensively. Help me to listen for the fear cloaked in blame. May I believe that your angel armies will protect me. Amen

Alone

> Then Elijah said to them: "I am the only one of the LORD's prophets left, but Baal has four hundred and fifty prophets." – *1 Kings 18:22*

Elijah is very good at remembering history. He is able to chronicle how things truly *went down*. He reminds Ahab that it was his fore-fathers turning away and worshiping other gods that led to the disastrous drought destroying the kingdom. And now Elijah says to the people, *I am the only one left*. It is like he calls out to the people asking, *where is your faith, where is your trust?*

Satan's greatest weapon is isolation. He can cloud our vision so that we see ourselves all alone. When we feel alone, we grab a hold of what we can control. Elijah acknowledges the odds. He stood up for God against 450 prophets of Baal.

The funny thing about loneliness is that you can feel it even when you are in a crowd of people. We can feel hard pressed on all sides, believing there are more people behaving badly than those living with integrity.

Do you ever feel alone? Do you wonder where God is in the midst of the culture life you live in?

Don't let Satan mislead you. God's people are all around. Pray that He will reveal one or two today.

Dear God,

Sometimes I feel outnumbered. I want to live for you with my whole being. I want to be your prophet. God show me who your people are and give me the courage to connect. Amen

Day 19

What is Your Idol?

> Then they called on the name of Baal from morning until noontime, shouting, "O Baal, answer us!" But there was no reply of any kind.
> – 1 Kings 18:26 NLT excerpt

In ancient times people believed in other gods. The god of Baal was the god of lightening, thunder, and rain. Isn't that funny? The very god they are yelling to hadn't answered them in three years. Baal isn't the ONE true God. He is a cheap substitute, just like my Discover, American Express, and Visa cards.

I trust my bank account, my own ability to control a situation, and my never-say-die work ethic. So often I find myself calling out: *O Credit Union, answer me* or *Oh time management tools, show me what to do.* I think we all do.

What is your idol? What do you rely on when things are tough? What distracts you from your trust in God?

Dear God,

Reveal my false gods. Please show me where I am trusting in the things of this world to fill me, complete me, or provide for me. God I want to trust you as my Protector and Provider. Amen

Rebuilding The Altar

With the stones he built an altar in the name of the LORD, and he dug a trench around it large enough to hold two seahs of seed. He arranged the wood, cut the bull into pieces and laid it on the wood. Then he said to them, "Fill four large jars with water and pour it on the offering and on the wood." ... the prophet Elijah stepped forward and prayed: "LORD, the God of Abraham, Isaac and Israel, *let it be known today that you are God in Israel* and that I am your servant and have done all these things at your command. Answer me, LORD, answer me, so these people will know that you, LORD, are God, and that you are turning their hearts back again."
– *1 Kings 18:32-37 emphasis added*

Elijah takes an active part in the reconstruction of the altar. He didn't throw the sacrificial calf on the ground, he asked his helpers to reassemble the resting place. He had them put the wood together and construct a foundation for the altar.

Sometimes I think God should pick up my collapsed corpse and rebuild it. And sometimes He does. But much of the time, He asks me to set my life back on the right path. The only way to re-establish my foundation is to fall on my knees. Recognizing my weakness and putting God first allows me to act according to my identity in Him. This process of confession, forgiveness, and foundation-setting answers the prayer: "Show the people that you, O Lord, are God."

What is an action step you can take to rebuild your foundation today?

Dear God,

Answer me, may I know that you are God. May you set my feet on the firm foundation of your truth, that I might see you holding me up. May you be the bedrock of my structure. Amen

Day 21

Why Does it Take a Miracle?

Then the fire of the LORD fell and burned up the sacrifice, the wood, the stones and the soil, and also licked up the water in the trench. When all the people saw this, they fell prostrate and cried, "The LORD—he is God! The LORD—he is God!"
– *1 Kings 18:38-39*

Why does it take a miracle for people to believe? Why does it take something miraculous for me to believe? I think it is because we are human. We are frail. We get distracted. We are attracted to shiny, twinkling, and sparkling objects. God wants us to see Him, not us. He wants us to give Him the glory for the miracle rather than credit ourselves.

Fire came from heaven. The soaking wet sacrifice was consumed by the flames. And when the people saw it they said: *The Lord—He is God!* There was no other explanation. They couldn't conjure it up. It was a miracle.

Where do you need a miracle today?

Dear God,

I need a miracle in my life today. I need to see you send fire from heaven. And I need my heart to be broken so that my only answer can be: "Lord—*You are* God!" Lord, be God in my life. Amen

The Rain is A'Coming

> And Elijah said to Ahab, "Go, eat and drink, for there is the sound of a heavy rain." So Ahab went off to eat and drink, but Elijah climbed to the top of Mount Carmel, bent down to the ground and put his face between his knees. – *1 Kings 18:41-42*

Elijah tells King Ahab, to take care of himself. He says go eat and drink because the *rain is coming*. Elijah takes a quick time out ... returning to the sight of the miracle. Elijah goes back to Mount Carmel and thanks God for providing fire. He doesn't stand with his hands raised to heaven ... basking in the knowing. Or confidently thank God for doing what he knew He would do. Instead Elijah bows down so low that he is almost in the fetal position. He is bent over with his face between his knees, praying. This is Elijah's awe inspired, humble response to God's glorious provision. Elijah has so much humility and awe of God's act of glory.

What do you do when God answers your prayers? What is your posture? Do you take credit? Do you think of all the "right" things you did to lead to the positive outcome? I do! Often I dismiss the miracle and it's Provider by taking credit for what I could control.

God reminds us that He is God and that we can have life altering, HUGE, unimaginable adventures by following Him. But like a father who saves nickels and dimes to buy his son a shiny red bike, He longs for the hug of gratitude from His child.

God longs for us to get low, bow down, and acknowledge His presence in our life.

Where is God present in your life today?

Dear God,

I lay my heart before you. I ask you to search me and know my in-most thoughts. Help me stay bowed down before you, recognizing your compassion, care, and unending LOVE. Amen

Small but Significant

"Go and look toward the sea," he told his servant. And
he went up and looked. "There is nothing there," he said.
Seven times Elijah said, "Go back." The seventh time the
servant reported, "A cloud as small as a man's hand is
rising from the sea." So Elijah said, "Go and tell Ahab,
'Hitch up your chariot and go down before the rain stops
you.'"
– 1 Kings 18:43-44

Seven is a perfect number. It is the number of completion.
Elijah's servant looked over the sea seven times
watching for something to happen. He trekked back and
forth messaging Elijah in person. There was no email or
instantaneous text message from his phone. Each time the
servant said: "There is nothing there." So, imagine his surprise
when on the seventh trip to the sea, he saw a small cloud the
size of a man's hand.

Ball up your fist, think of how small that is in the context
of the entire sky. God again begins His move with a small
gesture like a hand. The cloud indicates that God is changing
the weather. God signaled the weather with a tiny cloud. He
indicated He would answer the prayer for rain.

What is your fist-sized prayer for today?

Dear God,

I often look for the big things. I'm blinded by my big wants and miss the big needs you provide for me all the time. Today, Lord, help me see the small fist-size provisions you have for me. Amen

Day 24

Rain!

> Meanwhile, the sky grew black with clouds, the wind rose, a heavy rain started falling and Ahab rode off to Jezreel. The power of the LORD came on Elijah and, tucking his cloak into his belt, he ran ahead of Ahab all the way to Jezreel. Now Ahab told Jezebel everything Elijah had done and how he had killed all the prophets with the sword.
> *– 1 Kings 18:45-46, 19:1*

There is an old expression: *It's always darkest before the dawn.* Elijah's story takes a distressing turn. After the bright splash of fiery light from heaven came ominous clouds to darken the sky. It was not only black clouds but wind.

A spooky feeling often accompanies a big wind. The trees begin to creak, the windows of my house rattle, and I can even feel the earth move under my feet when a storm begins to brew.

Elijah knew the storm was coming. Elijah felt the storm coming. Elijah acted on the storm coming and he ran ahead of King Ahab to signal the end of the drought.

What do you do when you feel a storm coming? Do you react the same way when a storm in life heads your way? Do you lean into the storm or run away from it?

Dear God,

Help me to lean in and hold on to you when the storms of life
come my way. By holding on, help me see you in the midst of
the storm. Amen

The Death Wish

So Jezebel sent a messenger to Elijah to say, "May the gods deal with me, be it ever so severely, if by this time tomorrow I do not make your life like that of one of them." – 1 Kings 19:2

Elijah runs with super-human speed. You can almost feel the storm nipping at his heels. And in the midst of the run of his life Queen Jezebel's messenger meets him saying: *by this time tomorrow I will let the gods deal with me if you aren't dead.* Wow! That is the kind of message that will stop you in your tracks. God ... how are you going to work this out for me?

Have you ever been in the midst of making life changes, diligently obeying God, just to have something happen that seems to signal God has abandoned you?

This broken world we live in often collides with our Holy moments and seems to thwart them. Elijah obediently lives out God's directions and is met with a death threat by the queen. Did Elijah feel the hand of God settling him down? Or, did he feel alone, abandoned, and reminded of his past sins?

Today, when you feel unprotected, lean into the memory of God's past provision.

Dear God,

Help me when I can't help myself. Remind me of your provision when I feel unprotected. When I feel attacked, alone, and vulnerable, bring me peace, patience, gentleness, and self-control. Amen

Day 26

I'm Scared

Elijah was afraid and ran for his life ...
- 1 Kings 19:3

Fear is a powerful emotion. Satan's greatest weapon is to separate, isolate, and scare us. Elijah, the same man who told the widow: "do not be afraid," becomes so overwhelmed by Queen Jezebel's threat that he runs away in fear.

How do you act when you are afraid? Some of us become small, quiet, and withdrawn when we are threatened. Others of us puff up, become angry, bold, and bully others. Fear is a strong human emotion which cues into our feeling of being out of control.

What are you afraid of? If you are running from something God has told you, stop! If you are afraid to entertain an idea God has planted in your mind, look at it. If you are scared of losing, looking foolish, or being out of control, ask God to take the next step for you! *Rwanda?*

Dear God,

I am afraid. I know that when I feel scared I avoid resolving issues. I know I can't outrun this problem. Lord, open my hands and my heart to you. Please take my fear and replace it with your peace. I ask you for courage to take the next step on my journey. Amen

Choosing to be Alone!

When he came to Beersheba in Judah, he left his servant there, while he himself went a day's journey into the wilderness. – 1 Kings 19:3-4 excerpt

Remember Adam and Eve in the garden. They ate the fruit and hid. They were naked and ashamed when God came to walk with them in the cool of the day. Satan's greatest weapon is isolation. He convinces us that we are the only one who has ever felt this way.

It seems like Elijah steps right into Satan's territory when he leaves his servant behind. Now, I can see some positives to leaving your friend behind when you are furious and about to say a bunch of things in anger. And we don't know, maybe his servant wasn't trust worthy. But, what we do know is that Elijah set himself up when he kept running, alone. He finds himself in the wilderness – physically, emotionally, and spiritually dehydrated.

Close your eyes and count to 40. Picture a loved one's face. Spend a few minutes harvesting a support list. When you are physically, emotionally, and spiritually exhausted who do you go to? First, our help comes from the Lord and we should readily call on Him. Second, God created us for community and a good friend can lighten the load.

Dear God,

Grant me discernment as I create a support system. Guide me to godly people, who will give me Biblical advice and gentle support. Lord, thank you for creating me for community. Give me the courage to take a risk and reach out to a friend. Amen

Enough!

He came to a broom bush, sat down under it and prayed that he might die. "I have had ***enough***, LORD," he said. "Take my life; I am no better than my ancestors."
– 1 Kings 19:4 excerpt, emphasis added

Elijah was physically, emotionally, and spiritually exhausted. Instead of "always enough" He says to God: "I have had enough!" Elijah sat down under a broom tree and asked God to let him die. In this moment God seems not enough. The resurrection of the boy, always enough oil and flour, fire from heaven, protection from King Ahab's army, and the drought-ending rain are covered over by feelings of loneliness, exhaustion, and fear.

Elijah feels sad – so sad, scared, and alone that he asks God to let him die. Have you ever been there? Maybe you are there right now. You just can't see how He might turn this situation around. God gave us a host of emotions so that we could fully feel and interact with Him and His creation. If God created those feelings, He can comfort them as well.

Dear God,

If it is true that you created my feelings and see my emotions clearly ... help me make sense of them. I can't see through my tears, please wipe them away. Change my desire from: *Lord, I've had enough*, to: *Lord, you are enough.* Amen

*Caution—If you are feeling desperate and would like to hurt yourself, stop! Pick up the phone and call someone. Stay on the phone until you feel lighter or have connected with a mental health professional.

Day 29

Exhausted

Then he lay down under the tree and fell asleep. All at once an angel touched him and said, "Get up and eat." He looked around, and there by his head was some bread baked over hot coals, and a jar of water. He ate and drank and then lay down again. – *1 Kings 19:5-6*

There is an old adage that says: *Don't get too tired, too hungry, or too lonely.* Elijah is at this point – alone for a day's journey, physically exhausted, and feeling spiritually abandoned. After asking God to take his life, Elijah collapses under a broom tree and falls asleep.

Elijah has the guts to tell God what he is feeling. He cries out in desperation to God. When I read Elijah's words I feel the tension between what he knows he should say and what he wants to say. God doesn't say: "snap out of it ..." Instead, He asked him what he is doing there. And God, in His infinite grace, doesn't reprimand Elijah, He sends him an angel.

God sends Elijah a kind messenger. The angel physically touches Elijah, perhaps on his shoulder, almost to say: "I'm here! You are not alone." And then the angel directs Elijah to provision. There at his head is bread baking on hot coals and a jug of water to drink. And then the angel encourages Elijah to go back to sleep.

Maybe today you need an angel touch. Maybe you feel alone, worn out, unseen, and exhausted. God sends us angels unaware all the time. Just like Elijah woke up to a touch of provision, look around. Who touched you today? Did you see it? Did you recognize it as God breaking into your life?

Dear God,

Thank you for loving me so much that you would touch me on the shoulder and open my eyes to the provision right in front of me. Please help me SEE you today. Amen

Day 30

An Angel

The angel of the LORD came back a second time and touched him and said, "Get up and eat, for the journey is too much for you." So he got up and ate and drank. Strengthened by that food, he traveled forty days and forty nights until he reached Horeb, the mountain of God.
– *1 Kings 19:7-8*

One time wasn't enough. One touch from the angel wasn't enough. Maybe Elijah would have thought it was part of a dream. Maybe Elijah would have disregarded God's physical presence before him. So, God sent an angel a second time. The angel touched him again. And this time the angel directed him to eat, AGAIN.

God cares about our physical needs. He is concerned that we are taken care of. He reaches down into our reality and feeds our bellies, clothes us, and houses us. And He does it again, and again, and again. What a beautiful story.

God sends an angel a second time to touch Elijah, encouraging him to take care of himself, to eat, and to rest. Then God directs him on the next part of his journey. God doesn't always tell us our final destination but he does direct each step along the way.

What is your next step today?

Dear God,

Show me the next step on my journey. Reveal to me what you would have me do today. Give me the provision to get where you direct me to go. Amen

Day 31

"What are you doing here?"

There he went into a cave and spent the night. And the word of the LORD came to him: "What are you doing here, Elijah?" – 1 Kings 19:9

Elijah hears the word of the Lord. He hears God. God sends an angel to touch him, then He speaks to him again. There is an intimacy to God's question. He asks: "What are you doing here?" I feel the question reverberate off my soul. God directed him to the cave. Elijah had just complained and asked God to let him die. Now God says: "What are you doing here?"

I feel this question because I think God asks me sometimes: *Why are you here? Do you want to be here? Are you resenting what I've asked you to do? If you resent it, then what are you doing here?*

The psalmist says that God searches and knows our hearts. God already knows what Elijah is thinking and feeling, and yet He asks him anyway.

What are you doing here with God?

Dear God,

I ask questions like: *What am I doing here? Do I really trust you? Do you really see me? Will you really provide what I need?* Help me on my journey. Lord, be my Protector and Provider. Amen

Day 32

Poor Me!

He replied, "I have been very zealous for the LORD God Almighty. The Israelites have rejected your covenant, broken down your altars, and put your prophets to death with the sword. I am the only one left, and now they are trying to kill me too."
– 1 Kings 19:10

Poor Me! That is what Elijah says to God. He says: *Poor me. I have given you everything God, I was faithful, I am all alone … still following and now they want me dead.* I so get this sentiment. I often look around my life and complain: *Poor me! God, I have so much to do trying to convince these people to LOVE you.* The poor me sentiment doesn't really help anyone. Self-pity is indulgent and pitying others is degrading.

What are you questioning? Where do you think God has abandoned you? If He spoke to you, what would you want Him to say?

Dear God,

I am so selfish sometimes. I feel like I am the only one trying to be godly and in that I cast judgment and drive a wedge separating me from you all the more. God, I'm trying ... fill me up so I can love my neighbor, my co-worker, my kids, and my spouse, one more time. Amen

Look Up!

The LORD said, "Go out and stand on the mountain in the presence of the LORD, for the LORD is about to pass by." Then a great and powerful wind tore the mountains apart and shattered the rocks before the LORD, but the LORD was not in the wind. After the wind there was an earthquake, but the LORD was not in the earthquake. After the earthquake came a fire, but the LORD was not in the fire. And after the fire came a gentle whisper. When Elijah heard it, he pulled his cloak over his face and went out and stood at the mouth of the cave.
– 1 Kings 19:11-13 excerpt

God asked Elijah to get up, shake off his pity party, and step out to see God pass by. What an incredible invitation. The Living Lord urged Elijah to get up and come see Him. Elijah gets up and walks to the mouth of cave. He is suddenly overwhelmed by the sound of the wind. Just as the squealing subsides the mountain begins to tremble with an earthquake. And once he gets his footing back, fire rains down around him. This sounds spectacular, awe inspiring, and a little scary.

So, Elijah is overwhelmed by the noise, the movement, and the light ... then God whispers. The thing that moves Elijah most is the whisper. The whisper is so haunting he draws his cloak around him, covering his face as he stands at the mouth of the cave to hear more.

What do you need to silence in order to hear God's whisper today?

Dear God,

I want to know you more. Please help me slow down and quiet down so I can hear your whisper. Lord, let me hear your voice today. Amen

The Voice!

Then a voice said to him, "What are you doing here, Elijah?" – *1 Kings 19:13 excerpt*

I often look for God in the spectacular. But here God uses dazzling natural disasters as a prelude. He gets Elijah's attention. And then He whispers. He whispers a question to Elijah: "What are you doing here?"

Why did God ask Elijah the same question twice? Why does He want to know what Elijah is doing there?

I think God really wants Elijah to deeply know what he is doing there. I think God wants Elijah to stop and pay attention to his life calling. I think God desires Elijah's whole heart. I think God wants us to desire Him with our whole heart. He wants us to have a clear vision for our calling.

Are we going through the motions, or are we changing the world in His ways? Are we talking about peace and bringing peace wherever we go?

Dear God,

I stand before you again! Today, I ask you to fill me up. I ask you to guide me. I ask you to help me quiet down so that I can hear your whisper. And when I hear your whisper, Lord, grant me the courage to follow its instruction. Amen

Day 35

Poor Me ... Again!

He replied, "I have been very zealous for the LORD God Almighty. The Israelites have rejected your covenant, broken down your altars, and put your prophets to death with the sword. I am the only one left, and now they are trying to kill me too." The LORD said to him, "Go back the way you came, and go to the Desert of Damascus ... Yet I reserve seven thousand in Israel—all whose knees have not bowed down to Baal and whose mouths have not kissed him." – *1 Kings 19:14-15,18*

Elijah rehearses the same story a second time: *Oh God, poor me. I am all alone and they want to kill me.* God doesn't argue with Elijah. God doesn't try to talk him out of his feelings. He just reminds him that he is not alone: *Yet I have reserved seven thousand in Israel—all whose knees have not bowed down to Baal and whose mouths have not kissed him.* And God gives him new directions.

The Lord God Almighty directs Elijah to appoint new leaders and then sends him a friend, a mentee, a co-laborer, a companion, Elisha. This is an in-the-flesh representative of the seven thousand in Israel who did not follow Baal. God brought Elijah a God-fearing friend.

Pause, rest, and remember. The God of the Angel Armies is looking out for you. He will hear your cries and direct you to your next provision on the journey.

Do you have a friend for the journey?

Dear God,

I know I complain about the same thing over and over. Thank you for listening to me so patiently. Thank you for loving me. Thank you for directing me. Please help me to listen to your gentle voice. Amen

Two Times and Two Touches

And the word of the LORD came to him: "What are you doing here, Elijah?" ... Then a voice said to him, "What are you doing here, Elijah?" – *1 Kings 19:9,13 excerpt*

God asked Elijah twice: *Why are you here?* God's angel also touched Elijah two times in the wilderness. Why do we need two touches? I think that we are often so hung up with our own stuff – our worries, our needs, and our expectations – that we don't hear the answer the first time.

My three children often tell me stories. Sometimes I have just glanced at my phone and read a text message, or heard something provocative on the radio. They may have been talking for five minutes before I realize that I didn't hear a thing. It is not uncommon for me to say: *Can you tell me that again?* It is also not uncommon to hear me say: *Can you tell me that again in a different way? For some reason the information just didn't compute.*

I believe God questioned Elijah twice because Elijah is just like me. It seems as though Elijah's nonverbals said: *Can you tell me that again?* God verified that He heard Elijah. He asked him a second time.

God provided for him twice a day in the Kerith Valley, touched him twice in the wilderness, and questioned him twice on Mount Horeb. God was persistent and present. He was definitive and deliberate. God was Protector and Provider to Elijah.

Will you allow God to protect and provide for you?

Dear God,

Touch me twice. Tap my shoulder until I listen. Please help me to be quiet so that I can hear what you want me to hear, not what I want to hear. Amen

Day 37

But, There's Not Enough

All streams flow into the sea,
    yet the sea is never full.
To the place the streams come from,
    there they return again.
All things are wearisome,
    more than one can say.
The eye never has enough of seeing,
    nor the ear its fill of hearing.
What has been will be again,
    what has been done will be done again;
    there is nothing new under the sun.
– Ecclesiastes 1:7-9

His disciples answered, "Where could we get enough
bread in this remote place to feed such a crowd?"
– Matthew 15:33

Humans are comparative beings. From the time we are
young, we mentally and sometimes out loud express our
not enough. We didn't get as much as our sibling, our friend,
or our neighbor. Comparison cascades into scarcity thinking.
This type of thought tips us in the direction of self-sufficiency.

God designed us to be in communion with Him and others.
When we share, there is always enough. *Ecclesiastes* reminds
us that this is not the first time someone has felt wearisome. It
reminds us that what has happened before will happen again.
One side of the coin leads to scarcity and the notion that there
will always be suffering in this world. The flip side reminds
us that we are not alone. People have felt tired before us and
God provided what they needed. You feel tired right now, God

will provide enough of whatever you need – time, rest, food, friends. God is enough!

Where do you need God to *be enough* today?

Dear God,

I'm not sure how you can give me enough of what I need. I feel like the disciples when they asked how they could possibly feed the 5000 who gathered to hear Jesus. Thank you for reminding me that you fed 5000 with what seemed insignificant: two fish and five loaves of bread. Please help me see the *enough* for today. Amen

But, I'm Not Enough

> Then war broke out in heaven. Michael and his angels fought against the dragon, and the dragon and his angels fought back. But he was **not strong enough**, and they lost their place in heaven. The great dragon was hurled down—that ancient serpent called the devil, or Satan, who leads the whole world astray. He was hurled to the earth, and his angels with him. – *Revelation 12:7-9 emphasis added*

Even Elijah who courageously ran after God said: *I've had enough.* Throughout Scripture, God asks us to rely on His strength, not our own. *Revelation* chronicles the war between heaven and earth. The evil encapsulated in the dragon was not strong enough to defeat God. Michael and his angels were weighted with God's glory. They were glorious beings that could not be overpowered by the dragon.

Hebrews says we will be *weightier than the angels*. We have an opportunity to be filled, covered, and weighted with God's glory. In the Old Testament Isaiah said that when the glory of the Lord filled the temple no one could move. God's glory is heavy.

We can have this weight behind us, in us, and around us. This understanding of God's glory gives "being grounded" more power. This is why we are asked to stand up! When God's glory surrounds us, we can stand against incredible opposition, like Michael and the angels stood against the dragon. God's glory filled Elijah.

What are you standing up against today?

Dear God,

I know I'm not enough. In fact sometimes I side step what you have asked me to do, because I feel too small. Please help me to stand and wait for you to fill me. Lord, I love the picture of your glory being weighty and helping me stand my ground. I'm enough only when you are living within me. Amen

Day 39

God is Enough!

"What do you have against me, man of God? Did you
come to remind me of my sin and kill my son?"
– *1 Kings 17:18*

As high as heaven is over the earth,
  so strong is his love to those who fear him.
And as far as sunrise is from sunset,
  he has separated us from our sins.
– *Psalm 103:12 MSG*

The heart of the widow's cry is: *I know I'm not good
enough. I've been waiting for my past to creep up on me.*

I relate to the widow because I've spent years of my life
feeling not good enough. I'm not sure it is God I don't feel
good enough for. I think it is the comparison of my life with
others that often comes up short. Satan does an exquisite job
reminding of us of our past sins. He is remarkable at haunting
us with the worst reflection of ourselves. Satan wins when we
feel weak, insignificant, and not enough. When I believe that *I
am not enough,* I act like I am not enough.

And when I act like *I am not enough*, I sit on the sidelines
letting others represent God while I lick my wounds.

Brené Brown says: *We never have enough of what we don't
need.* The deep soul longing to love and be loved can only
be quenched by our Creator. Even the best love story here
on earth will leave us wanting for something. With God, our

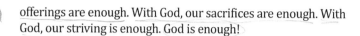

offerings are enough. With God, our sacrifices are enough. With God, our striving is enough. God is enough!

What haunting question keeps you from embracing that God is enough?

Dear God,

I surrender to your will for my life. Lord, I battle with memories of my past failings. I struggle to believe that you have truly loved me. Please, reach into the deepest part of my heart and free me from the fear of my past. Today, help me be a living expression that YOU are ENOUGH. Amen

Day 40

Always Enough

*Then the LORD said to Moses, "I will rain down bread from heaven for you. The people are to go out each day and gather **enough** for that day. In this way I will test them and see whether they will follow my instructions."*
– Exodus 16:4 emphasis added

Elijah isn't the first Biblical narrative to highlight the concept of "enough bread from heaven for today." God's Word is an incredible guidebook for living. The Israelite stories chronicle the behavioral pattern of God's people: they follow, they frustrate, they fall, and they follow through.

God provided Elijah just enough provision and protection for his journey. There was always enough flour and oil in the widow's jars. God showered bread from heaven – manna – long before Elijah, during the years Moses led the Israelites through the wilderness. And God rained bread from heaven when Jesus multiplied a little boy's loaves to feed 5000 people. God's provision is consistent, miraculous, and always enough!

Dear God,

You are consistent. You are true. And you are showing me I can trust you! I believe you will always be enough. Help me with my unbelief, when I feel I do not have enough. Amen

Made in the USA
Middletown, DE
06 February 2021